Washingt

BUSTLING
Beetles

by Peter Murray

™
sundance
A Haights Cross Communications ◂◂ Company

Sundance/Newbridge Educational Publishing, LLC
One Beeman Road
P.O. Box 740
Northborough, MA 01532-0740
800-343-8204
www.sundancepub.com

Adapted from *Naturebooks,* published in 2003 by The Child's World®, Inc.
P.O. Box 326
Chanhassen, MN 55317-0326

Photo Credits: Front cover, pp. 2, 9, 13, 17 © Robert and Linda Mitchell;
p. 6 © Adam Jones/Dembinsky Photo Assoc., Inc.; pp. 14, 29 © Bill Beatty/
Animals Animals; p. 18 © Jack Clark/Animals Animals; p. 21 (top) Anthony
Bannister, Gallo Images/Corbis; p. 21 (bottom) © Mark Moffett/Minden
Pictures; p. 22 © Ken Wagner/Visuals Unlimited; p. 25 © George Bryce/
Animals Animals; p. 26 © Michael P. Gadomski/Photo Researchers, Inc.;
p. 30 © Wolfgang Kaehler/Corbis; back cover, p. 10 © Bruce Davidson/
Animals Animals

ISBN 0-7608-9340-3

Printed in Canada

Contents

1 Meet the Beetle!

There is a kind of creature that lives almost everywhere. Turn over a rock, and you might find one of them. See them on the bark of trees. Notice them swimming in ponds. They might even be eating the vegetables in your garden. The more you look, the more you will find.

It's a beetle!

This milkweed beetle is resting on a milkweed plant.

Beetles are **insects.** The body of an insect has three parts. The front part is the head. The middle part is the **thorax,** or chest. And the back part is the abdomen. Insects have two eyes and **six legs.** They also have two **antennae,** which help them find food.

Most insects have two pairs of wings. The front wings are hard and act like **armor.** They protect the soft thorax of the insect. They also cover up its back wings and abdomen.

Notice the hard outer wings and soft inner wings of this longhorned beetle.

This goliath beetle is crawling
on a man's hand in Africa.

3 Are There Different Kinds?

One out of every five animals on Earth is a beetle. There are more than **300,000** kinds of beetles. Each kind, or **species,** is different.

Ladybugs are small. They are red with black spots. **Rhinoceros** beetles have long horns. They use their horns for fighting each other. Stag beetles have huge, pointed **jaws.** These beetles can grow to be over three inches long. Goliath beetles can grow even longer. They could **cover your face!**

That's one BIG beetle!

Beetles live **all over the world.** They make their homes in jungles, deserts, trees, and water. Some live on the ground. Some even live **under the ground.** You won't find them at the North or South Poles, though. It is too cold for them there.

Beautiful six-spotted scarab beetles like this one live in the jungles of Malaysia.

13

4 ▶ What Are Baby Beetles Like?

Beetles hatch from eggs. The baby **larva** looks like a little worm. The larva is very hungry. It eats a lot and grows fast. It sheds its skin many times so it can grow bigger.

Next the larva turns into a **pupa.** It stays this way for a few days or months. The pupa begins to change into its adult shape. This is also when its wings grow. The pupa sheds its skin one last time. It is now an adult! This change from egg to adult is called a **metamorphosis.**

These are the life stages of a beetle:
(1) egg (2) larva (3) pupa (4) adult.

5 What Do Beetles Eat?

Different beetles eat different foods. Tiger beetles eat small insects. Goliath beetles and stag beetles drink plant juices. Ladybugs eat insects that hurt plants. They help farmers and gardeners.

Not all beetles are this helpful. Some of them are pests. Snout beetles, or weevils, eat crops. Longhorned beetles eat their way through trees. Japanese beetles kill trees, bushes, and other plants.

This acorn weevil is feeding on an oak acorn.

Beetle larvae are always hungry. They need lots of food to grow. They eat flowers and crops. They even eat other insects. But some kinds like to **eat strange things.**

Meet the carpet beetle. Its larvae live in people's homes. They eat almost anything they can find. They eat feather pillows. They like wallpaper paste. They **nibble on** insulation. They even eat hot pepper powder!

Here you can see the larva of a carpet beetle.

Dung beetles lay their eggs in animal manure, or dung. They **roll the dung** into a ball. Then they bury it somewhere safe. After the eggs hatch, the larvae feed on the dung. They dig their way out when they get bigger.

The larvae of tiger beetles live in holes. Only their large jaws show above the ground. They wait for insects to come near. Then they grab the insects and eat them!

It's a lousy job, but someone's got to do it!

Top Photo: These dung beetles are guarding a ball of dung.

Bottom Photo: Tiger beetle larvae live underground.

6 Do Beetles Have Enemies?

Many animals eat beetles. Birds, frogs, and spiders eat them. So do **snakes,** fish, and some insects. Sometimes farmers have too many beetles. Then they just bring in another insect *to eat them!*

Japanese beetles were once eating too many crops in the United States. Scientists found an insect that liked to eat the beetles. The spring Tiphia wasp was called in. The wasps saved the crops!

Japanese beetles are pests to farmers.

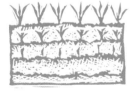

7 How Do Beetles Stay Safe?

Beetles have many tricks for staying alive. Bombardier beetles are kind of like skunks. They have a special way of fighting back. First the enemy hears a **loud pop.** Then the beetle shoots out a hot liquid. It smells bad! A puff of smoke even comes out. The enemy thinks twice before trying to eat a bombardier beetle again!

I think I'm in love with a beetle.

This bombardier beetle is crawling on a beach.

Many beetles are helpless on their backs. But not the click beetle! It rolls onto its back to **trick its enemy.** It pretends to be dead. Later, the beetle bends its body and snaps it back. With a loud "click!" it flips into the air and lands on its feet.

The eyed click beetle has another trick. It uses **mimicry** to fool the enemy. It has spots that look like **big eyes.** Hungry birds and frogs pass it by. They think it is a larger animal.

Notice the eyelike markings on this eyed click beetle.

8 ▸ Are Beetles Dangerous?

Most beetles are **harmless** to people. But there are some that people should stay away from. The **blister** beetle is one of them. It can give you blisters on your skin. The stag beetle is another. It might *pinch you* with its jaws. Beetles just want to eat and lay their eggs. They like to be left alone.

Here you can easily see the jaws of this stag beetle.

9 ▸ Are Beetles in Danger?

Beetles are **pretty successful** insects. They can live almost anywhere. Still, some of them are in danger. The places where these beetles live are being **destroyed.**

Beetles are an important part of our world. Take a **look around** the next time you are outside. See how many kinds of beetles you can spot. You might be surprised!

Rhinoceros beetles like this one live in the rain forests—areas in danger of being destroyed.

Glossary

antennae long feelers on an insect's head that help it to find food

larva (larvae) young insect(s) between the egg stage and the pupa stage of life

metamorphosis a series of changes some animals go through from egg to adult

mimicry the ability to look or act like something else

pupa a young insect at the stage of life when its body changes into an adult's

species different kinds of an animal

thorax an insect's chest area

Index